SPECIAL REPORTS

THE 2016 PRESIDENTIAL ELECTION

BY TOM STREISSGUTH

CONTENT CONSULTANT
Elizabeth P. Klages, PhD
Department of Political Science
Normandale Community College

Essential Library
An Imprint of Abdo Publishing | abdopublishing.com

abdopublishing.com

Published by Abdo Publishing, a division of ABDO, PO Box 398166, Minneapolis, Minnesota 55439. Copyright © 2018 by Abdo Consulting Group, Inc. International copyrights reserved in all countries. No part of this book may be reproduced in any form without written permission from the publisher. Essential Library™ is a trademark and logo of Abdo Publishing.

Printed in the United States of America, North Mankato, Minnesota
102017
012018

Cover Photo: Julio Cortez/AP Images
Interior Photos: Erica Yoon/The Roanoke Times/AP Images, 4–5; Anthony Behar/Sipa/AP Images, 7; Julie Jacobson/AP Images, 9; Christopher Gregory/Getty Images News/Getty Images, 12–13; Bebeto Matthews/AP Images, 15; Saul Loeb/AP Images, 19; Richard B. Levine/Newscom, 22–23; MediaPunch/REX/Shutterstock/AP Images, 26; Rick Friedman/Corbis News/Getty Images, 30; Robert F. Bukaty/AP Images, 33; Dennis Van Tine/MediaPunch/IPX/AP Images, 36–37; Justin Sullivan/Getty Images News/Getty Images, 40–41; David Zalubowski/AP Images, 44; Darron Cummings/AP Images, 47; Matt Rourke/AP Images, 48–49; David Hume Kennerly/Archive Photos/Getty Images, 53; J. Scott Applewhite/AP Images, 55; Ron Sachs/picture-alliance/dpa/AP Images, 56; Tom Williams/CQ Roll Call/AP Images, 60–61; Manuel Balce Ceneta/AP Images, 65; Josh Edelson/AFP/Getty Images, 67; Brynn Anderson/AP Images, 68–69; Mary Altaffer/AP Images, 74; Cliff Owen/AP Images, 78; Andrew Harnik/AP Images, 80–81; Ed Reinke/AP Images, 84; Dan Callister/Rex Features/Shutterstock/AP Images, 87; Red Line Editorial, 90–91; Olivier Douliery/Sipa USA/AP Images, 92–93; Jose Luis Magana/AP Images, 98

Editor: Arnold Ringstad
Series Designer: Maggie Villaume

Publisher's Cataloging-in-Publication Data

Names: Streissguth, Tom, author.
Title: The 2016 presidential election / by Tom Streissguth.
Description: Minneapolis, Minnesota : Abdo Publishing, 2018. | Series: Special reports | Includes bibliographic references and index.
Identifiers: LCCN 2017946915 | ISBN 9781532113369 (lib.bdg.) | ISBN 9781532152245 (ebook)
Subjects: LCSH: Presidents--Election--Juvenile literature. | United States--Juvenile literature. | Presidential candidates--Juvenile literature. | Political and social views--Juvenile literature.
Classification: DDC 324.973091--dc23
LC record available at https://lccn.loc.gov/2017946915

CONTENTS

TWO PARTIES
IN NEW YORK

t is the evening of November 8, 2016—Election Day in the United States. Earlier in the day, tens of millions of people traveled to schools, community centers, libraries, city halls, and churches to cast their votes for president. Now the results are streaming in from across the country.

The presidential election is one of the biggest events in American civic life. Like soccer's World Cup or the Summer Olympics, it comes around every four years. For months or even years leading up to the vote, the election dominates the print and broadcast media.

Since announcing their runs for president in early 2015, the two major-party candidates had made speeches, held rallies, and given interviews. They

The long, arduous campaign for president came down to individual decisions in voting booths across the country.

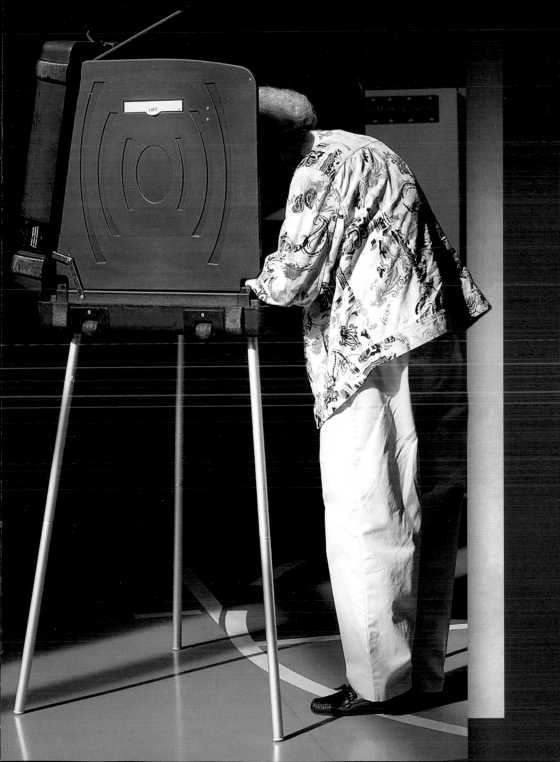

PRESIDENTIAL REQUIREMENTS

To run for president, no specific experience is needed. However, the US Constitution does lay out a few requirements. A candidate must be at least 35 years old. He or she must be a natural-born US citizen. The candidate also must have resided in the United States for at least 14 years.

Once candidates have collected $5,000 in contributions for their campaigns, they have 15 days to file a Statement of Candidacy with the Federal Election Commission. This process authorizes an official campaign committee. Within ten days, the committee must file a Statement of Organization. Throughout the campaign, the committee must report every dollar it receives and spends.

each made the case that they were the right choice for one of the world's toughest jobs. Democratic Party candidate Hillary Clinton said her long experience in government had prepared her for the White House. Republican Party candidate Donald Trump said he was a skilled businessman who knew how to negotiate the great deals the country needed.

In New York City, the two contenders wait for the results. For the last two years they have traveled thousands of miles. Their campaigns spent millions of dollars contributed by corporations, unions, nonprofit groups, and individual supporters. Now, as maps of the vote tally light up television monitors, they are just a few miles apart. Clinton supporters are at the Javits Center, and Trump's team is at the Midtown Hilton. Confident of victory, Clinton

Crowds of Clinton supporters wait for election results at the Javits Center.

scheduled a victory party at the Peninsula Hotel, just one block from Trump's home at Trump Tower.

The first results come in around 7:30 p.m. As each voting precinct makes the count, it reports the results to the Associated Press (AP). This news organization then submits the numbers to the major broadcast networks, who then present the tallies to their viewers. All day long, polltakers have been questioning voters as they leave voting places. The networks use these early evening exit polls, combined with the later AP results, to predict a winner in each state. This lets them determine the likely winner as soon as possible.

The system of reporting results brings a suspenseful night as viewers wait for the projected winner of each state. A media outlet that correctly projects a winner first scores an important victory. One that projects the wrong candidate suffers an embarrassing setback.

FIRST RESULTS

The AP calls its first state winners around 7:05 p.m., eastern time. Trump will win Indiana and Kentucky, and Clinton will win Vermont. The suspense continues as results arrive from the crucial swing states, toss-up states which could realistically be won by either candidate. Around 10:30, Ohio—which has voted for the winner in every election since 1964—is called for Trump. Approximately 20 minutes later, Trump takes Florida, then North Carolina.

Trump supporters, wearing duplicates of their candidate's trademark red cap, await election results in New York City.

Nevertheless, Clinton is winning the New England states, as well as New Jersey and New York, a state which alone gives her 29 electoral votes.

These electoral votes are the real deciders in any presidential election. In the United States, the votes of ordinary citizens do not directly elect the president. Instead, a majority of the 538 votes of the Electoral College awards the presidency. That means the threshold of victory is 270 electoral votes. Each state has a set number of electors, and they typically cast their electoral votes for the popular vote winner in their state.

The voting in many states is so close that it's impossible to project a winner until the early morning of the next day. At 12:34 a.m., the state of New Hampshire, for example, has tallied 278,905 votes for Trump and 278,890 votes for Clinton. In this New England state, just 15 votes separate the candidates.[1]

But with many states voting reliably Democratic or Republican, the swing states are the real battleground. The two candidates have campaigned heavily in Ohio, Pennsylvania, Florida, North Carolina, and Virginia. They're also paying

DISAPPEARING POLLS

The Voting Rights Act of 1965 put some states, mostly in the South, on notice. The law declared that these states were discriminating against voters on the basis of race. If these states wanted to change their election laws, they would have to apply to the federal government for approval.

An important Supreme Court decision in 2013 struck down parts of the Voting Rights Act. This decision meant states could shrink the number of polling places. With fewer polling places open, it becomes harder for people to vote. In particular, critics said that the closures made it tougher for African Americans, Hispanics, and other racial minorities—who often vote Democratic—to cast their votes.

Maricopa County, Arizona, shut down 140 polling places. This allowed only one polling place for every 21,000 voters in the county in 2016. In the entire state of Arizona, 212 polling places were shut down. Texas led the nation in polling place closures with 403. Louisiana shut down 103, followed by Alabama (66), Mississippi (44), North Carolina (27), and South Carolina (12).[2]

close attention to Michigan. Although Michigan has cast its 16 electoral votes for the Democratic candidate in every election since 1992, the polls in that state this year are very close.

Late into the evening, news reports describe Michigan as too close to call. The same is true for Wisconsin. Another key state, Pennsylvania, also seems to be holding out into the early morning. With a win in Pennsylvania, either candidate can claim a clear path to eventual victory. Trump has been racking up an impressive list of swing state victories. But Clinton has campaigned heavily in Pennsylvania, holding a rally in Philadelphia on the day before the election. She can also expect the western states of Oregon, Washington, and California to break her way.

> "WE WENT INTO THE NIGHT KNOWING THERE WAS A CHANCE TRUMP COULD WIN. BUT ALL THE SMART PEOPLE SAID IT WAS NOT GOING TO HAPPEN."[3]
>
> **—TELEVISION NEWS ANCHOR JUDY WOODRUFF**

At 1:39 in the morning of November 9, the AP reports that the state of Pennsylvania has finally declared a winner. The election of 2016, after a campaign stretching back a year and a half, has finally been decided.

CHAPTER TWO

RIDING
THE GOLDEN
ESCALATOR

Trump Tower rises more than 50 stories along one of the busiest stretches of Fifth Avenue in New York City. On this midtown Manhattan street, the traffic runs heavy. Pedestrians bustle among expensive hotels and glamorous, beautifully appointed shops. It's not easy for anyone to draw much attention. But on June 15, 2015, as he rode down a brightly gilded escalator to Trump Tower's lobby, Donald J. Trump managed it with ease.

A crowd of supporters had already gathered. They cheered with enthusiasm as Trump gave a thumbs-up and his wife, Melania, smiled and waved. Trump then

Trump rode down a golden escalator to Trump Tower's lobby to announce his presidential campaign.

took the podium for an important announcement. He began speaking about the loss of American prestige, economic strength, and jobs. He complained about politicians in Washington, DC, and he complained that the country just wasn't winning against China, Japan, and Mexico:

> Our country is in serious trouble. We don't have victories anymore. We used to have victories, but we don't have them. When was the last time anybody saw us beating, let's say, China in a trade deal? They kill us. I beat China all the time. All the time.[1]

MIXED REVIEWS

In his speech, Trump also declared he'd be paying for the campaign himself. "I'm using my own money," he said, to loud cheers. "I'm not using lobbyists. I'm not using donors. I don't care. I'm really rich."[2] That meant he wouldn't be taking any donations from the wealthy. Nor would he be owing any favors to the political establishment in Washington. He promised he was just what the country needed.

Trump was not the first to announce his candidacy for the 2016 presidential election. But the theme of his kickoff

Unlike many of his Republican rivals, Trump entered the campaign with a nationally known brand name.

speech set him apart. He said he was a winner, plain and simple. His long experience as a successful businessman, Trump explained, had taught him how to cut great deals. He could face down any foreign leader and negotiate his way to a better American future, one deal at a time.

As a candidate, Trump also spoke about immigrants, who have played a role in American politics since the country's beginnings. He took a serious interest in Mexico, commenting on the illegal immigrants coming across the southern border. "They're not sending their best," he said, to applause and shouts from the crowd. "They're not sending you. They're not sending you. They're sending

"I WOULD BUILD A GREAT WALL, AND NOBODY BUILDS WALLS BETTER THAN ME, BELIEVE ME, AND I'LL BUILD THEM VERY INEXPENSIVELY. I WILL BUILD A GREAT, GREAT WALL ON OUR SOUTHERN BORDER. AND I WILL HAVE MEXICO PAY FOR THAT WALL."[4]

—DONALD TRUMP, JUNE 16, 2015

people that have lots of problems, and they're bringing those problems with us. They're bringing drugs. They're bringing crime. They're rapists. And some, I assume, are good people."[3]

The performance got national attention in the print and broadcast media. Many people were upset at his characterization of immigrants as "rapists." Some writers pointed out that Trump was a political amateur who had never held elected office. Most commentators treated his campaign as a personal whim, if not a joke. Over a grueling campaign that would last for another 16 months, they claimed, the novelty of his candidacy would wear off and his popularity would wane.

THE MIDDLE OF THE ROAD

Trump had been famous for decades, with his name and image prominent in the media. But his more experienced opponents had already run, and won, campaigns for state and federal office. Reporters and newspaper columnists opined that these mainstream politicians would eventually catch up to Trump's celebrity. They would offer a more serious discussion of important issues, such as the economy, health care, and immigration. They would tear Trump apart in the televised debates—despite his undeniable skill in front of cameras, honed during his years as a reality show star.

A great example of such a mainstream candidate was Jeb Bush, the brother of President George W. Bush and son of President George H. W. Bush. Bush announced his candidacy in June 2015. Bush was the favorite of wealthy Republican

THE FIRST GO-ROUND

Donald Trump had considered running for president before. In early 2011, while starring in the reality television show *The Apprentice*, he had declared himself a Republican candidate for president. He had the difficult task of running against an incumbent president: Barack Obama.

In the political world, Trump was best known for raising the issue of Obama's birthplace. He declared that the president's "short-form" birth certificate might be fake, making Obama ineligible to be president under the rules of the Constitution. There was no evidence to support Trump's assertion. After Obama produced a copy of his original "long-form" birth certificate, however, the issue died. Still, for years afterward, Trump refused to admit he had been wrong.

Shortly afterward, Trump withdrew from the 2012 race. "I have spent the past several months unofficially campaigning and recognize that running for public office cannot be done half-heartedly. Ultimately, however, business is my greatest passion and I am not ready to leave the private sector."[5] Obama's defeat of Republican Mitt Romney in the 2012 election inspired Trump to try again in 2016.

donors seeking to defeat the expected Democratic Party candidate, Hillary Clinton.

Other Republican candidates seeking the nomination jumped into the field as 2015 continued. Marco Rubio, a Florida senator, appealed to the growing Hispanic electorate with his Cuban heritage and to Republicans with his strong conservative stance on many issues. Texas senator Ted Cruz also had a strong national following in the Republican Party, and he had made a name for himself by staunchly opposing President Barack Obama's policies in the US Senate. Carly Fiorina, the only woman running for the Republican nomination, had been a chief executive officer of Hewlett-Packard, a large technology company. In all, 17 Republicans eventually announced candidacies, making it one of the most crowded presidential fields in history. The huge group of candidates would be narrowed in the primary campaign, in which party supporters in each state vote for their favorite candidates. After the party chose its general election candidate, this person would face off against the Democratic Party's candidate.

The Republicans had a big obstacle in Hillary Clinton, the front-runner for the Democratic Party's nomination.

As secretary of state, Clinton met with a wide variety of world leaders, including German chancellor Angela Merkel.

Clinton brought long political experience to the campaign. The wife of President Bill Clinton, she had already spent eight years in the White House as First Lady between 1993 and 2001. She was best known at that time for heading a group that proposed reforms to the country's health insurance system.

Although her broader changes were not passed in Congress, Clinton did successfully promote the Children's Health Insurance Program, which remains an important federal program. In 2000, she was elected as a senator for New York, and in 2009 she was appointed secretary of state by newly elected President Barack Obama.

Clinton's Republican opponents pointed to controversies that arose during Clinton's career. They brought up her work at the Clinton Foundation. The Foundation formed partnerships between private business and government to address issues such as climate change, public health, and economic development. Opponents of Clinton claimed, however, that the foundation was used as a means to raise money and reward donors with political favors through Clinton's job at the Department of State.

Trump had public relations problems of his own. He had a long history of business failures and controversial statements, especially regarding women and minorities. He had been involved in thousands of business lawsuits, brought by people who claimed he didn't pay his bills or stick to his contracts. A lawsuit was still pending, for example, against Trump University. This school was supposed to teach its

ENDORSEMENTS

Hillary Clinton gathered endorsements from prominent Democrats including Governor Jerry Brown of California and Representative Nancy Pelosi, leader of the Democrats in the House of Representatives. In past elections, such endorsements were valuable in swaying the voters. Hillary also had a big supporter in President Barack Obama. With the help of the popular President Obama, Hillary Clinton was favored by most to win the presidential election in 2016.

students how to become successful real estate investors. Many Trump University students, however, claimed it was a scam.

To many in the media, Trump also had an awkward way of appearing unprepared for his speeches and public appearances. But for his growing legion of fans, the Trump style was a refreshing change from the stiff, formal speech of conventional politicians. Instead, Trump spoke bluntly. He made a simple promise to the voters, summed up in a slogan that appeared on posters, signs, T-shirts, and his signature red ball cap: "Make America Great Again."

THE START OF A SLOGAN

Just a few days after Obama's victory over his Republican opponent, Mitt Romney, in the presidential election of 2012, Trump was considering a run for president. He needed a catchy phrase or slogan that would capture the public's imagination. "Make America Great" didn't seem quite right. "We Will Make America Great" didn't work, either. Finally, Trump came up with "Make America Great Again."[6] It wasn't too long or short, and it was easy to remember.

Trump immediately had his lawyers take the needed steps to file for trademark protection. In about a month, the US Patent and Trademark office approved Application No. 85783371, Registration Number 4773272, for "Political action committee services, namely, promoting public awareness of political issues."[7] With the trademark, the Trump campaign can legally deny the use of the phrase to anyone else in order to promote a political campaign.

CHAPTER THREE

THE FRONT-RUNNER

O n April 12, 2015, Hillary Clinton announced her candidacy for president. Instead of making a grand speech in a big public venue, she chose a new format: a YouTube video. She appealed to voters with an argument for economic fairness: "Americans have fought their way back from tough economic times, but the deck is still stacked in favor of those at the top."[1]

Clinton was well prepared. She had a lot of experience in Washington. She had worked on health-care legislation during the 1990s presidency of her husband, Bill. She had served as a senator from New

Supporters around the country watched Clinton launch her campaign on smartphones, tablets, and computers.

York from 2001 to 2009 and as secretary of state during President Obama's first term, from 2009 to 2013. She had also run for president in 2008, losing the Democratic nomination to Obama, who was then a senator from Illinois. For her 2016 run, Clinton underlined her experience in the legislature and her work for women's rights and reform of the health insurance system.

Supporters liked Clinton's support for environmental protection and her desire to combat global climate change. They agreed with her plans to continue and expand the health insurance reforms started by President Obama. Her proposed reforms in law enforcement and the justice system were designed to improve racial equality in the country. Supporters also liked her economic policies, such as increased taxes on wealthy individuals and corporations and more support for Americans in poverty. This support would include cheaper college education and additional funding for Social Security, a program that provides income to retired Americans. Clinton supporters felt her proposals fit with her campaign slogan: "Stronger Together."

PUTTING A CAMPAIGN TOGETHER

Clinton had other circumstances working in her favor. There seemed to be no major contenders on the Democratic side. Nor did the Republican Party have a strong leading candidate to challenge her. She was popular with college-educated women, African Americans, and Hispanics, as well as among labor union leaders. She also had wide name recognition, a critical asset for anyone running for national office. The Clinton campaign had already established a headquarters in New York City, and a donor network was raising plenty of money.

Clinton, like other candidates, had to worry a lot about money. In a presidential campaign, it's not enough to be rich. A lot of money is needed, more than a single individual—except for perhaps a billionaire—can afford. Candidates have to put together networks of donors who are willing to write big checks, hold fund-raising events and parties, recruit other donors, and help with organizing

"IT'S OUTRAGEOUS THAT MULTI-MILLIONAIRES AND BILLIONAIRES ARE ALLOWED TO PLAY BY A DIFFERENT SET OF RULES THAN HARDWORKING FAMILIES, ESPECIALLY WHEN IT COMES TO PAYING THEIR FAIR SHARE OF TAXES."[2]

—HILLARY CLINTON, JANUARY 11, 2016

25

Clinton's campaign centered around her slogan, "Stronger Together."

state-level campaigns. Also necessary are political action committees (PACs).

The purpose of a PAC is to organize in support of an issue or political cause. By the time Hillary Clinton announced her candidacy, her PACs, including Ready for Hillary and Priorities USA Action, were raising millions of dollars and preparing to buy advertising to market her to the voters.

ON THE ROAD

Soon after her announcement, Clinton hit the campaign trail in a Chevrolet Express van, driving from New York to Iowa to meet and greet ordinary voters. She stopped along the way to talk with people in restaurants and other public places. She avoided the press, however.

Along the route from New York to the Midwest, there were no press conferences, events at which reporters gather and ask questions in an unscripted setting.

Clinton finally agreed to answer a few questions from reporters on May 19 in Cedar Falls, Iowa. One of them asked about Clinton's vote as a senator to authorize the US invasion of Iraq and the overthrow of Iraq's leader, Saddam Hussein, in 2003. Clinton said she had "made a mistake plain and simple."[3]

A couple of questions were also raised about Clinton's use of e-mail as secretary of state. A congressional investigating committee had discovered that Clinton had set up a private server in her home to handle

WHAT'S A TOWN HALL?

Republican and Democratic candidates took part in a long series of town hall meetings throughout the 2016 campaign season. The tradition goes all the way back to 1633, when the first town hall was held in Dorchester, Massachusetts. Every Monday at 8:00 a.m., the citizens of Dorchester had a chance to gather in a local meeting house and discuss their problems. Any decisions they agreed to by majority vote had the force of law.

At a modern town hall, ordinary citizens have a chance to ask questions and engage in a conversation with political candidates. Town halls occur at all levels of politics, but only presidential town halls enjoy nationwide, live coverage on television. The first took place in 1992, when Governor Bill Clinton of Arkansas persuaded President George H. W. Bush to try the format. Clinton had a talent for talking to ordinary people, and knew he would shine in a format very different from a formal debate. He was right. The town halls were key in propelling Clinton to nationwide popularity and his eventual victory over Bush.

MORE TO THE
STORY

PACS AND SUPER PACS

In 1944, the Congress of Industrial Organizations (CIO) formed a campaign committee to help reelect President Franklin Roosevelt. An association of labor unions, the CIO saw Roosevelt as the best candidate to support unionized workers. This was the country's first political action committee (PAC). The committee accepted donations from workers at a time when unions were barred from supporting political campaigns. Because the funds came from workers rather than the union, this support did not violate the law.

Since then, PACs have become the most important way for presidential campaigns to promote their candidates and raise money for advertising. In the past, federal law limited donations from, and contributions to, political action committees. For example, PACs could donate $5,000 to a candidate's committee, as well as $15,000 a year to a party committee. They could also accept up to $5,000 from individuals, party committees, or other PACs.

Two important Supreme Court decisions in 2010, *SpeechNow.org v. Federal Election Commission* and *Citizens United v. Federal Election Commission*, brought a change to the PAC rules. The independent expenditure-only committee, or Super PAC, was born. These groups cannot donate money directly to a candidate or coordinate their activities with a candidate's campaign. But there's no limit on the amount of money they can accept from individuals, corporations, or unions, and no limit on what they can spend. For the 2016 elections, 2,389 Super PACs were formed. They received $1,790,933,772 in donations and spent $1,104,481,088. The largest by far was Priorities USA Action, which spent $133,407,972 in support of Clinton and her allies in the Democratic Party.[4]

her work e-mails. This raised security questions, as a set of strict rules governs the handling of classified material within federal departments. Opponents in Congress and the media were now demanding that Clinton's e-mails be released from the US Department of State.

MONEY AND POLITICS

Iowa was a key early focus for any candidate. On February 1, 2016, it would be the site of Democratic and Republican caucuses. These meetings hold the first vote of any kind on each party's presidential nominees. A win in Iowa doesn't ensure the nomination of the party. But it does give the victor crucial momentum in the race. This is important for drawing more donations from supporters.

In her speeches, Clinton targeted middle-class voters who saw their own wages stagnate as the top earners took an ever-larger share of income. She pointed out the basic unfairness of wealthy people paying a lower share of their income in taxes than the average worker. She also discussed income inequality between men and women. Clinton announced she was in favor of reforming the campaign finance system. This system made running for

Sanders was popular in his home state and quickly attracted a passionate following for his presidential campaign.

president a matter of raising enormous amounts of money from wealthy individuals and large corporations.

On this theme, Clinton and her main rival, Vermont senator Bernie Sanders, could agree. Sanders had announced his candidacy on April 30, 2015, just two weeks after Clinton's YouTube video. He was a self-described socialist and independent, though he chose to run for the Democratic Party's presidential nomination. With no previous ties to either major political party, he seemed to be a long shot. Some believed he was just seeking the national political spotlight to express his views.

But Sanders was an experienced politician, and he was very persistent. Before winning his first elected office as mayor of Burlington, Vermont, he had lost several campaigns in a row. Now he spelled out his grievances against the country's economic inequalities in much sharper tones than did Clinton. This brought him attention from the start of his campaign.

SEVENTEEN CHALLENGERS

The Republican Party's 17 candidates were all considered long shots to beat Hillary Clinton. None of these hopefuls had Clinton's name recognition or her fund-raising power. They also lacked majority support among Republican voters.

More popular names emerged through the spring and summer. In addition to Jeb Bush, Governor Scott Walker of Wisconsin announced his candidacy. Walker had become

TO RUN OR NOT TO RUN

The Democratic Party had two official candidates by the fall of 2015. In the meantime, a third candidate—Vice President Joe Biden—was waiting for the right moment to announce. Biden hinted in interviews that he was interested in running, and he had formed a network of friends he could count on to help with a campaign. But the decision was a hard one. He was a close ally of Clinton and knew that his own candidacy would probably attract more primary voters from her than from Sanders. Running a campaign also takes total dedication and a lot of energy. At this time, Biden and his family were grieving over the loss of his son, Beau Biden, to cancer earlier in the year. There are some hard deadlines in a presidential run. In the fall of the year before the election, the candidate must begin filing paperwork to get on state primary ballots. Missing this deadline blocks the candidate from claiming state delegates to the nominating conventions. Committees must be organized in each state, and money must be raised. Facing these obstacles, on October 21 Biden announced he would not run in 2016.

a household name across the country after a 2011 legal dispute with his state's public employee unions. A new law, 2011 Wisconsin Act 10, made changes to the way the unions worked. One of its provisions was that it limited collective bargaining, meaning that it would be harder for unions to negotiate for better wages. Walker's Republican supporters cheered the change, while his Democratic opponents were harshly opposed to it. Walker survived a recall election, in which the voters can attempt to remove a sitting governor and force a special election to replace him or her.

Bush had plenty of donors and a campaign organization ready to handle a presidential run. But he was unimpressive on the campaign trail. Setting himself out as the calm, rational choice against Trump, to many people Bush's serious speaking style made him sound bored and boring. Not all Republican voters were enthusiastic about having yet another member of the Bush family in the White House. Bush was seen as part of the establishment. The troubled presidency of Jeb's brother George W. Bush prompted Republican voters to seek an alternative and a clean break with the past.

The Republicans relied on the public perception that they were stronger on foreign affairs and military issues. But presidential candidates must be mindful of public opinion. Bush did not want to run against the widespread opposition to the Iraq War (2003–2011), which had been started by his brother. He avoided the subject of the war in his public appearances, instead promising a successful fight against the militant group Islamic State in Iraq and Syria (ISIS), which had risen in Iraq after the war had ended.

SOCIAL CONSERVATIVES AND TED CRUZ

Bush may have been confident of his standing in the crowded Republican field. But he was also facing a rising wave of enthusiasm for Trump as well as the surging candidacy of Senator Cruz of Texas. Through the

Bush had originally been seen as a front-runner, but he began to fade as the long campaign continued.

summer and fall of 2015, Cruz gained support among the Republican Party's social conservatives, who felt passionately about issues such as gay marriage, abortion, gun rights, and religion.

Cruz and his Republican opponents had a chance to share their views at the first Republican debate on August 6, 2015. The debate featured ten candidates. A separate debate was held on the same day for the seven candidates with lower poll numbers.

The debates continued in a long series through the fall. Trump's poll numbers held strong, and more experienced politicians such as Bush began dropping out of the race. Although the Republican candidates bickered, talked over one another, and argued with the debate moderators, their overall message was clear. They believed the presidency of Barack Obama had been a failure, and they said the country needed new, more conservative leadership.

MORE TO THE
STORY

AN EASY PROMISE

Candidates often criticize laws they don't like. If they can't find
a way to change the law, they often suggest something easier
said than done: changing the US Constitution. During the Republican
campaign, presidential hopefuls suggested several amendments—
even though a president has no formal role in the process. A
balanced budget amendment was one favorite. This would force
the US Congress to stop running budget deficits and ensure that
the federal government spends no more than it receives in taxes.
A term limits amendment, which would limit the number of terms
members of the Senate and House of Representatives may serve,
also found favor. Republicans also responded to a Supreme Court
decision allowing same-sex marriage by proposing a marriage
amendment. This would allow states to pass laws declaring that a
legal marriage can only take place between a man and a woman.

Amending the Constitution isn't as easy as proposing
amendments, however. The US Congress must pass the amendment
by a two-thirds majority in both the House of Representatives and
the Senate. Alternately, two-thirds of the state legislatures can
propose an amendment. Three-quarters of the states must then
pass the amendment. The last amendment to survive this process
was the 27th, which passed in 1992. This amendment states that
a change in the salaries of Congress cannot take effect until after
the next election.

CHAPTER FOUR

THE PRIMARY
SEASON

Through the winter and spring of election year, the states hold primaries and caucuses. Through these minor elections, voters cast ballots for their favored candidate in a primary, or they attend a meeting of party members in a caucus. The excitement builds as the primaries gradually bring the most popular candidates to the top. Winners of each election gain a portion of the party's national delegates. Whoever gets the most delegates will become the nominee. After all the primaries and caucuses are over, the delegates meet at the national

Candidates descend upon Iowa to make their pitches to voters before the critical first caucus of primary season.

A PRIMER ON PRIMARIES

The primary system began in the early 1900s. In the 1800s, party leaders gathered every four years to choose their presidential nominee in a secret ballot. There was no way for ordinary voters to take part in this process. The Progressive era in politics, which began in the late 1800s, saw a drive among voters to change this system, which was known for bribery and underhanded deal making. Seeking a more democratic, open way to choose their candidates, the two major parties began holding statewide votes for delegates, who would then vote at nominating conventions. The first presidential primary took place in 1901 in Florida.

party conventions to formally select the party's nominee.

Primary season kicks off with the Iowa caucuses. In 2016, the caucuses took place on February 1. Democratic and Republican Party members in 1,681 precincts met to talk, argue, and listen to speeches.[1] At the end of the Republican caucuses, those in attendance cast secret ballots for their preferred candidate. The results were then tallied for the entire state.

The Democratic caucuses had a slightly different format. As soon as the meeting began, each attendee stated his or her preferred candidate. Those who backed the same candidate clustered in a staked-out portion of the room. If a group didn't meet a particular threshold, usually 15 percent, its members were released to join a more popular group.[2] Then a second vote took place.

The votes were not secret—everyone had to declare their choice publicly.

A CLOSE NIGHT

Not everyone in Iowa bothers to attend a caucus. In the depths of a cold winter, it takes commitment to show up to a political meeting. But the Iowa voters know their caucuses are crucial—the first winner of primary season can use the victory to raise money from donors. Little-known candidates can emerge as legitimate contenders. In 2008, Obama's enthusiastic Iowa supporters shocked the Democratic side by turning out in large numbers. The win over Clinton gave Obama's campaign an important boost that would carry him through the primary season.

In 2016, the Iowa caucuses put Clinton ahead of Sanders by a slim margin, winning 49.9 to 49.6 percent. On the Republican side, Cruz edged out Trump with a 27.7 to 24.3 percent victory.[3] Rubio came in third. The result solidified Cruz's position as a front-runner in the Republican race.

FROM THE
HEADLINES

GIVING SPEECHES, MAKING MONEY

During the 2016 campaign, Hillary Clinton drew criticism from both parties for making a lot of money from speeches. Since 2001, Bill and Hillary Clinton gave 729 speeches, earning an average of $210,795 for each. Hillary also earned $1.8 million for giving speeches to big banks—a problem for critics who believed that, as president, she would work in their interest.[4]

The Clintons weren't the only politicians to make out well as public speakers. Former presidents can earn hundreds of thousands of dollars for a single speech. President George W. Bush, for example, earns $100,000 to $175,000 for a speech.[5] President Barack Obama, after leaving office in 2017, agreed to take $400,000 for talking to Cantor Fitzgerald, an investment bank.[6] Also in demand are candidates who drop from the race before the election or who lose the nomination.

Public speaking is a big business. The Washington Speakers Bureau represents politicians and other notable people, including

Many former politicians, including President Bill Clinton, have made large amounts of money speaking for corporate clients.

astronauts, retired military officers, and business executives. The bureau collects a fee for arranging speeches by its many clients. It also negotiates the topic to be discussed and the type of talk to be given. Critics will often point out that presidential candidates might be in the race just to boost their public profiles, their media exposure, and the speaker fees they can command.

The primaries continued, state by state, through the winter and spring. The states have varying rules on voting. Some allow any eligible voter to take part, while others restrict the voting to party members. Some award delegates in proportion to the percentage of votes won by a candidate, while others award all of the delegates to the winner. Although the Iowa caucuses boosted the Cruz campaign, a wave started for Trump after a win in New Hampshire's proportional primary vote. Once dismissed as an unserious candidate simply doing it for the media attention, Trump went on to victory in Nevada, South Carolina, and Alabama.

On the Democratic side, Sanders won New Hampshire, an expected result in his home

MARCO RUBIO

Florida senator Marco Rubio was one of the Republican Party's rising young stars in 2016. The son of Cuban immigrants, he appealed to Hispanic Republican voters. Florida offered 29 electoral votes and had been a crucial swing state in recent elections. But Rubio had supported an immigration bill that was strongly opposed by conservative Republicans. The bill had provided immigrants a path to citizenship, allowing them to eventually gain legal status without returning to their home countries. For his initial support of this law, Rubio was now considered soft on immigration.

During the presidential campaign, Rubio would try to overcome the controversy by claiming the bill was never meant to pass. "The Senate immigration law was not headed towards becoming law," he declared at a campaign stop in South Carolina. "Ideally, it was headed towards the House, where conservative members of the House were going to make it even better."[7]

region of New England. Clinton, who ran strong in the South, came out on top through South Carolina, Alabama, and Arkansas before losing by a big margin to Sanders in Colorado. The close race encouraged Sanders's millions of donors to keep giving. In February, the Sanders campaign raised $42 million. In March, Sanders hit a new monthly record of $46 million as the Clinton campaign raised less than half of that, $21 million.[8]

SUPER TUESDAY

As each new primary takes place, delegate totals add up for the leaders. The candidates who are lagging behind begin to drop out of the race. Rubio won his first and only state primary in Minnesota, while Cruz survived the Trump onslaught by winning Oklahoma and his home state of Texas.

On March 1, a date known as Super Tuesday, 13 states held primaries or caucuses. By the time of these elections, Trump was dominating the Republican field. His potential nomination began to worry a group of more traditional Republican leaders. They formed a Never Trump movement to rally opposition within the party.

Voters crowded schools, churches, and other voting locations for primaries and caucuses on Super Tuesday.

The Never Trump movement had a problem: it needed a candidate to rally around, but there was no single candidate with a clear shot to beat Trump. Cruz and Rubio were both running a close second in the polls, and neither was willing to drop out of the race. The three-way race fractured the opposition to Trump, and Trump positioned himself as the true outsider.

Trump and Sanders made strong gains among primary voters. Trump had a habit of improvising speeches, and audiences cheered wildly for his spontaneous style. Sanders raised millions in small donations, presenting himself as the candidate of young people and workers. Unhappy with conventional politicians, many voters cast their ballots against the party establishment on both sides.

THE NARROWING FIELD

Through February and March, the Republican primaries delivered more victories to Trump, who began pulling away from Cruz and Rubio. Unable to win a clear lead in any state, Rubio dropped out of the race in March. Around the same time, John Kasich emerged as a leader of the moderate Republicans. As the governor of Ohio, he promised to deliver not only experience but also an important swing state. Kasich, however, could not come near Trump's vote totals and only carried the Ohio primary.

On the Democratic side, Sanders scored some wins and ran close to Clinton in the delegate count. The Sanders campaign seemed to be gaining some momentum, but the way to the nomination was blocked by the Democratic superdelegates. These are prominent members of the Democratic Party, including governors and members of Congress. A group known as the Hunt Commission created the process for choosing superdelegates in 1981. Superdelegates are not bound by primary voting and can vote for the candidate of their choice at the convention. There are 714 superdelegates out of 4,765 total Democratic delegates.[9] The majority of these superdelegates supported Hillary Clinton.

WE HAVE A WINNER

For the Republicans, the moment of truth arrived with the Indiana primary on May 3. Winning the 57 convention delegates at stake would deliver an unstoppable lead of delegates to Trump. Both pro- and anti-Trump forces spent heavily on televised advertising in the state. Anti-Trump PACs and candidates spent $2.8 million, the Cruz campaign spent $3.3 million, and Trump's campaign spent less than $1 million.[10] Cruz won the endorsement of Indiana governor Mike Pence. Additionally, he tried to bolster his campaign by naming Carly Fiorina, who had dropped out of the race, as his running mate.

Trump repeated a newspaper tabloid story that

"A RACIST COMMENT"

Many people were troubled by a situation that followed a lawsuit filed against Trump University. Assigned to handle the case was Judge Gonzalo Curiel of the Southern California District Court. Curiel's Mexican heritage, Trump claimed, meant the judge couldn't be fair in the case. Even Republican Speaker of the House Paul Ryan criticized this as a "textbook definition of a racist comment."[11] Curiel urged the two sides to settle the case rather than try it before a jury. Eventually, Trump agreed to a settlement in which he paid $25 million to the 3,730 Trump University students who brought their claims to court.[12]

claimed Cruz's father was somehow involved in the assassination of President John F. Kennedy in 1963. Katie Packer, the chair of Our Principles, an anti-Trump PAC, said, "There is more than a month before the California primary—more time for Trump to continue to disqualify himself in the eyes of voters, as he did yet again spreading absurd tabloid lies about Ted Cruz's father and the JFK assassination."[13]

Trump voters were not deterred. Their candidate spoke his mind without the careful style that can make ordinary political speeches vague and dull. From May through the final primaries held on June 7 in California, Montana, New Jersey, New Mexico, North Dakota, and South Dakota, Trump won every delegate at stake. This gave Trump a clear path to the nomination—if he could avoid defections and a floor fight at the Republican National Convention in July.

Cruz named Carly Fiorina as his vice presidential candidate in a last-ditch effort to kick-start his campaign.

CHAPTER FIVE

THE
CONVENTIONS

The two parties hold their national conventions in the summer. For a few days, each party advertises its candidates, sets out its platform, and puts on a show for the television audience. Everything is planned, down to the last minute. Over the course of three days, the convention builds to its highlight: a speech by the candidate, accepting the nomination and promising to win big in November.

At one time, nominations were decided at the conventions. Republican and Democratic delegates held a series of votes to pick the candidate. If there was no clear winner, more votes would take place, sometimes long into the night.

The parties' national conventions are huge, flashy media events.

BROKERED CONVENTIONS

Modern political conventions feature little suspense over who will be the nominee. By the time the parties gather, primary contests have decided the nomination well in advance. The last brokered convention occurred in 1952. On the Republican side, Senator Robert Taft was in a close contest with Dwight D. Eisenhower. Taft had won 2.8 million votes during the primaries to 2 million for Eisenhower.[1] But party leaders believed Eisenhower, a popular figure who had served as a general in World War II (1939–1945), had a better chance to win the general election. As the 1952 Republican convention began in Chicago, Illinois, the eventual winner was uncertain.

At this time only approximately one quarter of the states held primaries or caucuses. Most of the delegates were unpledged to one candidate or the other. Powerful party leaders, including governors Thomas Dewey of New York and Earl Warren of California, controlled these unbound delegates. Meeting among themselves, they agreed to throw their support to Eisenhower, who went on to win the nomination and the presidency.

By 2016, however, this practice was only a memory. The major parties don't want to show disagreement, indecisiveness, or any opposition among party members to their nominees. Nor do they want a long series of ballots dragging into the early morning. The primary season now decides who the nominees will be far in advance of the conventions.

A CONVENTION IN CLEVELAND

Trump held a majority of delegates by the time of the Republican convention in Cleveland, Ohio. Just before the start of the convention, he announced his running mate: Governor Mike Pence of Indiana. Pence was an experienced politician favored by the social conservatives who had supported Cruz. Nevertheless, there were many in the party who still opposed Trump's nomination.

Just before the convention, a Rules Committee of the Republican National Committee met to hammer out some important details. The anti-Trump party members had a plan: convince the group to change the rules to allow delegates to vote against Trump. In this way, Cruz, Kasich, or another Trump alternative might be able to win the nomination.

The Rules Committee heard pleas from both sides. Trump opponents declared that delegates should be able to vote as they wished. Supporters demanded the delegates obey the will of primary voters. The decision came on July 14, a few days before the convention opened. Delegates would have to vote for the primary winners.

TED CRUZ

The decision in the Rules Committee paved a clear path for Trump to win the Republican nomination. But the front-runner was still making controversial statements.

At one town hall meeting in July, Trump targeted Arizona senator John McCain, one of his critics. A veteran of the Vietnam War (1954–1975), McCain had been held prisoner for more than five years during the conflict. "He's not a war hero," said Trump. "He was a war hero because he was captured. I like people who weren't captured."[2] It was a slap to prisoners of war, who are typically shown great respect and honor for their service.

In Cleveland, Trump failed to win important endorsements from Republican leaders. Nor could he persuade them to show up at the convention and speak on his behalf. Although Cruz agreed to deliver a prime-time speech, Bush—along with the rest of his family—stayed home, as did Kasich.

The convention planners did bring several prominent supporters to Cleveland, including actor Scott Baio and reality television star Omarosa Manigault, who had appeared on Trump's TV series *The Apprentice*. Trump's wife, sons, and daughter Ivanka also gave the candidate warm endorsements.

Senator Cruz's speech angered Trump backers when the senator refused to mention Trump's name. "Please,

Trump's speech was the climax of the four-day convention.

don't stay home in November," said the senator. "If you love our country, and love your children as much as I know that you do, stand, and speak, and vote your conscience."[3]

Trump himself spoke on the night of July 21, the last day of the convention. In his speech, he described "chaos" and "violence" in the United States, blaming much of this on illegal immigrants. He also said that US citizens were going through "international humiliation" as a result of Obama's foreign policy. He said that he could "make America great again" through stricter crime enforcement and immigration policies. Speaking of what he described as a corrupt political system, he said, "Nobody knows the system better than me, which is why I alone can fix it."[4]

THE DEMOCRATIC NATIONAL CONVENTION

The Democratic National Convention went more smoothly for Clinton. By the opening day of the event, Sanders had endorsed her. Although Sanders had won 22 primaries or caucuses over the year and drawn 13 million votes, Clinton had a clear lead in delegates. She also had the support of most superdelegates.

But many Sanders supporters were not ready to follow his lead. Some declared their intention to write in Sanders's name on the November presidential ballot. Others were leaning toward Trump or to third-party candidates, such as Jill Stein of the Green Party or Gary Johnson of the Libertarian Party. Trump tried to appeal to Sanders voters who saw Clinton as part of the Washington establishment.

The convention began on July 25 in Philadelphia, one week following the Republican convention. President Obama, First Lady Michelle Obama, Bill Clinton, and Joe Biden gave speeches in support of Hillary Clinton, as did her choice for vice president, Governor Tim Kaine of

Following Khan's speech, Trump criticized the grieving couple, igniting a media controversy.

Virginia. One memorable speech was given by a Pakistani American lawyer, Khizr Khan, against Donald Trump. He stood beside his wife, Ghazala, onstage. The father of a US soldier killed in Iraq, Khan brandished a small blue booklet, asking Trump, "Have you even read the US Constitution? I will gladly lend you my copy. In this document, look

for the words 'liberty' and 'equal protection of law.'"[5]

The party platform mentioned policies advanced by the Sanders campaign. It called for a raise in the minimum wage to $15 an hour, an expansion of Social Security benefits, and the abolition of the death penalty.

Clinton spoke on the last night of the convention. In her speech, she thanked Sanders for bringing economic and social justice issues to the forefront of the campaign. She criticized the tone and content of Trump's convention speech, saying, "He wants to divide us from the rest of the world, and from each other." Clinton spoke of the need for compassionate immigration reforms and an economic policy that "works for everyone, not just those at the top." She also highlighted the historical significance of her candidacy:

"THE CHOICE IS CLEAR, MY FRIENDS. EVERY GENERATION OF AMERICANS HAS COME TOGETHER TO MAKE OUR COUNTRY FREER, FAIRER AND STRONGER. NONE OF US EVER HAVE OR CAN DO IT ALONE. I KNOW THAT AT A TIME WHEN SO MUCH SEEMS TO BE PULLING US APART, IT CAN BE HARD TO IMAGINE HOW WE'LL EVER PULL TOGETHER. BUT I'M HERE TO TELL YOU TONIGHT—PROGRESS IS POSSIBLE."[6]

—HILLARY CLINTON, FROM HER CONVENTION SPEECH

Clinton's convention speech emphasized her experience in government.

Standing here, standing here as my mother's daughter, and my daughter's mother, I'm so happy this day has come. I'm happy for grandmothers and little girls and everyone in between. I'm happy for boys and men, too—because when any barrier falls in America, it clears the way for everyone. After all, when there are no ceilings, the sky's the limit.[7]

E-MAIL PROBLEMS

Although Clinton had won endorsements from Democratic leaders, controversy once again erupted over e-mails. More than 19,000 messages hacked from the Democratic National Committee (DNC) were published online on July 22.[8] The messages were posted by WikiLeaks, an organization that releases secret or classified information leaked to it by hackers or government insiders. The e-mails revealed that members of the DNC favored Clinton over Sanders. Supporters of Sanders pointed to the messages as evidence that top party officials had conspired against their candidate.

But the convention, and the glowing speeches of support from Democratic leaders, gave Clinton a bump in the polls. With a clear lead over Trump, who had several controversies of his own to handle, the

Democratic nominee seemed well positioned for a win in November. With the two candidates officially chosen, it was finally time for the general election campaign to begin.

ALSO RUNNING

The federal election law doesn't restrict a presidential run to members of the two major parties. But in order to run an effective national campaign, the funding networks and support of a major party are necessary. A Republican or Democrat has won every presidential election since 1848, when Zachary Taylor triumphed as a member of the Whig party.

That doesn't stop people from trying. In 2016, hundreds of people filed papers with the Federal Election Commission to run for president. Two of them would gain significant attention in the media: Gary Johnson of the Libertarian Party and Jill Stein of the Green Party.

CHAPTER SIX

THE GENERAL
CAMPAIGN

A fter the nominating conventions, the presidential campaign swung into its final phase. Trump and Clinton had three months to show they were prepared for one of the most difficult and complex jobs in the world. With no need to compete against other candidates from their own parties, the nominees now were raising more money. By August, Clinton had a wide lead over Trump in donations. She was also spending much more than Trump on television advertising.

THE ELECTORAL MAP

In the general election, the electoral college decides the winner. A total of 270 votes are needed for victory.

Clinton campaigned alongside Joe Biden at a rally in Pennsylvania a few weeks after the nominating convention.

In some states, the polls showed Clinton and Trump running even, with just one or two percentage points separating them. In other states one candidate had a reliable margin. California, for example, had voted for the Democratic candidate in every election since 1988—and its 55 electoral votes were the most of any state. Clinton could also count on New York, her home state, which had 29 electoral votes. Other Democratic strongholds included Oregon, New Jersey, Massachusetts, and Minnesota.

Trump had widespread support in the South, including Texas with its 36 electoral votes. Reliable Republican votes could also be found in the Mountain West states of Idaho, Montana, and Wyoming. The Great Plains states of Nebraska, Kansas, Oklahoma, and the Dakotas generally voted Republican. For campaign strategists, the

THE ELECTORAL COLLEGE: WHY?

The US Constitution set down the rules for presidential elections. The framers of the Constitution debated the wisdom of using a nationwide popular vote or having representatives in Congress cast the deciding votes. They didn't like either idea. The Electoral College was a compromise.

Why not simply use the popular vote? There was a problem: communications were poor and slow in the 1700s, when the US Constitution was written. Not knowing much about national candidates, the voters might simply vote for somebody from their own state. The result would be several candidates getting votes, but none a majority. In this case, only the largest states with the most voters would be deciding on the future president.

most important states were the swing states, where the polls were close and the outcome unpredictable. These included Pennsylvania, North Carolina, Virginia, and Ohio. The candidates made frequent stops in the swing states. They targeted television advertising to swing-state voters in order to gain an edge.

DUELING SCANDALS

In their public appearances, the candidates talked about pressing public issues, such as immigration. While Trump wanted to ban Muslims from immigrating to the United States, Clinton wanted a path to citizenship for immigrants entering the country illegally. While Trump wanted to cut business taxes, Clinton favored higher tax rates on the wealthy. Trump called global warming a hoax and promised to pull the United States out of global climate agreements. Clinton said that as president, she would hold to the agreements and vowed to increase renewable energy use.

"DONALD J. TRUMP IS CALLING FOR A TOTAL AND COMPLETE SHUTDOWN OF MUSLIMS ENTERING THE UNITED STATES UNTIL OUR COUNTRY'S REPRESENTATIVES CAN FIGURE OUT WHAT IS GOING ON."[1]

—DONALD TRUMP,
DECEMBER 7, 2015

The candidates also talked about each other. In their advertising, they emphasized their own virtues and the opponent's faults. The voters were treated to a stream of negative ads produced by the campaigns and by the PACs that supported them. In negative ads, the goal is to tear down the opponent.

Clinton often spoke of Trump's past business history, pointing out that Trump hadn't always had the great successes he claimed. In fact, several of Trump's ventures had failed, and four of his companies had declared bankruptcy. Clinton had other questions about Trump's financial history. She demanded, for example, that he release his tax returns to the public. Presidential candidates do this routinely. The documents show in detail how an individual or company earns and spends money. They also show how much someone claims to have given to charity. Trump, however, refused to comply.

During a debate, Clinton raised the question again. "Maybe he's not as rich as he says he is," she commented. "Maybe he's not as charitable as he claims to be. . . . Or maybe he doesn't want the American people, all of you

Many citizens demanded that Trump release his tax returns to make his financial history clearer.

watching tonight, to know that he paid nothing in federal taxes."[2]

Trump had a few questions to raise as well. In campaign speeches, he often mentioned the Clinton Foundation. Some donors to the charity met with Clinton in her official position as secretary of state. In addition, several countries had donated to the foundation. The government of Saudi Arabia, for example, gave the foundation $10 million.[3] Critics asked whether such donations were meant as a way to gain favor with the US government.

The Clinton Foundation became another awkward subject for Clinton. To answer the questions raised, the Clintons announced in August that, should Hillary win the election, the foundation would no longer accept donations from foreign individuals or corporations.

The personal attacks and the accusation of corruption still proved useful for Trump. Since he had never held an elected office, nobody could accuse him of working for his own interest in public office. Clinton, on the other hand, had held office for more than a decade. During that time, her performance was under constant scrutiny by the press and the public. Trump could easily bring that spotlight to bear.

PROBLEMS WITH PERCEPTION

Clinton criticized Trump's blustery, bragging style, hinting often that he was not the right man for the job of president. How could a businessman, she asked, separate his private affairs from his work as president? Would a President Trump work for the voters who elected him? Or would he simply use his position as the leader of the United States to make more money for himself?

Trump shrugged off the attacks. He suggested business experience was just what the country needed. In his view, both Democratic and Republican politicians

Trump's supporters followed their candidate in attacking Clinton's history.

had mismanaged the federal government for a long time. Trump claimed his abilities as a dealmaker would allow him to serve more effectively in the White House.

The media gave less attention to issues such as climate change, the tax system, a reform of the immigration laws, economic development, or military strategy. In general, serious policy discussions don't hold the public's interest as much as verbal combat on a more personal level. In addition, television networks thrive on insults, scandals, and controversy, which boost their audience and their revenues.

CHAPTER SEVEN

STATUS QUO
VERSUS
UPSTART

Although Clinton kept a lead in national opinion polls taken by news agencies, Trump's message resonated among many voters. The crowds greeted Trump with loud cheers in the Rust Belt, the Midwestern states hit hard by the loss of manufacturing jobs since the 1980s. On September 14, Trump spoke in Canton, Ohio. As at most of his campaign stops, he followed no script. But the themes and ideas were the same as at all of his other rallies.

At Canton, Trump lamented the decline in good-paying manufacturing jobs. Ford had just announced a move of some factory production

At rallies around the country, Trump found large, supportive crowds.

to Mexico. Trump now promised severe punishment: a 35 percent tax on every car brought into the United States from abroad. The subject of immigration also came up. In his speech, Trump made a promise that undocumented foreigners streaming into the country would be stopped. He would build an enormous border wall, running from the Gulf of Mexico to the Pacific, to prevent more illegal immigration.

ISSUES: IMMIGRATION

One of the big issues in the 2016 campaign was immigration. The candidates each had strong opinions on how best to change the immigration laws and deal with the arrival of unauthorized foreigners across the borders. The issue was especially important to residents of border states, such as New Mexico, Arizona, and Texas.

Clinton and the Democrats favored a more compassionate system of immigration laws and a path to citizenship for undocumented immigrants. The Republicans favored tighter security along the borders and a wall that would prevent illegal border crossings from Mexico. Trump promised to force Mexico to pay for the wall and said he would order the deportation of the estimated 11 million illegal immigrants.[1] Clinton said she wouldn't be interested in mass deportations.

DEBATE NIGHTS

The candidates participated in three presidential debates. In any campaign, debates are crucial events. Instead of speaking to an audience limited by the size of a hall or arena, candidates have the chance to reach out to millions of television viewers. With a single well-chosen and memorable phrase, they can cut an opponent down and convince voters they are presidential material. Stumbling through a debate question, however, can have the opposite effect—a loss of face and poor marks from the public and the press. The first debate between Clinton and Trump took place on September 26 at Hofstra University in New York. The event drew 84 million television viewers—an all-time record for presidential debates.[2] Opinion polls found that a majority of viewers felt Clinton won all three debates.

Every debate has a theme. For the first debate in 2016, the theme was the economy and jobs. As the first speaker to answer a question from moderator Lester Holt, Clinton explained her plan for growing the economy: public investment. By spending money, governments can stimulate the economy and create jobs building roads and bridges. "We also have to make the economy fairer," she declared. "That starts with raising the national minimum

"I WANT US TO INVEST IN YOU. I WANT US TO INVEST IN YOUR FUTURE. THAT MEANS JOBS IN INFRASTRUCTURE, IN ADVANCED MANUFACTURING, INNOVATION AND TECHNOLOGY, CLEAN, RENEWABLE ENERGY, AND SMALL BUSINESS, BECAUSE MOST OF THE NEW JOBS WILL COME FROM SMALL BUSINESS."[3]

—HILLARY CLINTON TO VIEWERS OF THE FIRST PRESIDENTIAL DEBATE, SEPTEMBER 26, 2016

wage and also guarantee, finally, equal pay for women's work."[4]

Trump took a different approach. He would depend on the private sector to create new jobs. He would also negotiate better trade deals. Foreign countries such as China and Mexico were beating the United States, he said, and he would bring this to a stop. His answer to the problem was simple: "Under my plan, I'll be reducing taxes tremendously, from 35 percent to 15 percent for companies, small and big businesses. That's going to be a job creator like we haven't seen since Ronald Reagan. It's going to be a beautiful thing to watch."[5]

But questions about Trump's character arose to drown out other messages. On October 7, an 11-year-old tape of Trump bantering with Billy Bush from the television show *Access Hollywood* emerged. On the tape, Trump and Bush could be heard making lewd comments about women. The outrage that followed prompted Trump to make an apology, while Melania came forward to dismiss the comments as "boy talk."[7]

Two more debates followed. During the second debate, on the subject of terrorism, Trump made a promise: "I will knock the hell out of ISIS. . . . I will tell you, I will take care of ISIS."[8] Clinton also spoke about ISIS, emphasizing her differences with Trump in engaging with the nations of the Middle East. She suggested that Trump's inflammatory remarks about Muslims would harm the effort to beat ISIS: "I intend to defeat ISIS, to do so in a coalition with majority Muslim nations. Right now, a lot of those nations are hearing what Donald says and wondering, why should we cooperate with the Americans? And this is a gift to ISIS and the terrorists, violent jihadist terrorists."[9]

ISSUES: THE ECONOMY

By the summer of 2016, the US economy was growing, but slowly. Wages were stagnant and didn't seem to keep pace with the cost of living. Clinton emphasized more economic opportunity for women and minorities, a rise in the minimum wage, and higher taxes on the wealthy. The Trump campaign offered a simpler solution: tax cuts for businesses. The thinking was that such cuts would spur new investment. Trump also promised to tear up foreign trade deals, such as the North American Free Trade Agreement, and remove the US from the newer Trans-Pacific Partnership (a stance that Clinton agreed with). By renegotiating these deals, Trump promised to boost the sales of US goods abroad.

The third debate, in Las Vegas, Nevada, featured

talk on gun rights, abortion, and immigration. Clinton

supported women's rights to abortion services, citing the

Supreme Court case *Roe v. Wade*: "I strongly support *Roe v.*

Wade, which guarantees a constitutional right to a woman

to make the most intimate, most difficult, in many cases,

decisions about her health care that one can imagine."

Trump responded by asserting, "Well, I think it's terrible. If

you go with what Hillary is saying, in the ninth month, you

can take the baby and rip the baby out of the womb of the

mother just prior to the birth of the baby." Clinton accused

him of mischaracterizing the issue and using "scare

The candidates talked about both personal and policy issues during the debates.

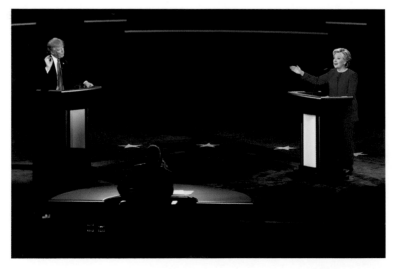

rhetoric."[10] The topic of Russia also came up. Pointing out Trump's open admiration for Russian president Vladimir Putin, Clinton called Trump a Russian puppet. "It is pretty clear you won't admit that the Russians have engaged in cyber attacks against the United States of America," she added.[11]

In fact, intelligence agencies in the United States had already discovered that hackers allied with the Russian government had broken into e-mail servers at the DNC. The Russians were now ensuring the e-mails were released in an attempt to turn public opinion against Clinton and support Trump's campaign. As Election Day neared, the pace of these e-mail releases increased. This was not the limit of Russian interference. In August and September, Russian hackers also attempted to hack into American voter databases in many states.

AN E-MAIL CONTROVERSY

Clinton's use of a private e-mail server resulted in her opponents accusing her of mishandling classified documents and risking national security. They also suggested the e-mails would reveal shady dealings.

In fact, Clinton has skirted rules requiring her to keep e-mail records at the State Department. In 2015, soon after the use of the server was revealed, she apologized for the practice and admitted it was a mistake. On facing questions from the press, she said she had used the server for convenience and to keep sensitive documents protected from hacking. "What I had done was allowed, it was above board," she stated in a September 2015 interview. "But in retrospect, certainly, as I look back at it now, even though it was allowed, I should've used two accounts. One for personal, one for work-related e-mails. That was a mistake. I'm sorry about that. I take responsibility."[12] In a debate with Sanders in February 2016, she said she had not sent or received classified information over the server.

The server issue did not go away with Clinton's apologies. In the summer of 2016, the Federal Bureau of Investigation (FBI) started an investigation into the situation. A federal employee mishandling classified documents is a criminal matter. FBI director James Comey stated that a total of 110 e-mails sent to and from Clinton contained some form of classified information, and he said, "There is evidence that they were extremely careless in their handling of very sensitive, highly classified information."[13] Nevertheless, the FBI cleared Clinton and her colleagues at the Department of State of any intentional wrongdoing.

That was not quite good enough for Trump. He returned to the subject often on the campaign trail. There were still e-mails to be found, he claimed, and he even encouraged foreign hackers to retrieve them: "I will tell you this, Russia: If you're listening, I hope you're able to find the 30,000 e-mails that are missing. I think you will probably be rewarded mightily by our press."[14] Both candidates had been briefed by US intelligence agencies

Comey became an important figure in the campaign following his statement in the summer of 2016.

on the hacking of DNC servers and the theft of e-mails. Investigators had discovered that the software used was identical to that used by Russian agents to sway elections in other countries.

In the final days of the fall campaign season, Clinton was leading in the polls. But then, the issue of e-mail came back to the public's attention. On October 28, the FBI announced that it would be continuing its investigation into Hillary Clinton's e-mail use. In a letter to Congress signed by Comey, the director stated, "In connection with an unrelated case, the FBI has learned of the existence of e-mails that appear to be pertinent to the investigation."[15] The FBI would examine the e-mails to see if they contained classified information.

The letter from Comey broke into newspaper headlines and television news programs. It brought the e-mail issue back to the attention of the voters. It was now less than two weeks before Election Day. Trump pounced on the news, praising the FBI's action at a rally in New Hampshire: "Hillary Clinton's corruption is on a scale we have never seen before. We must not let her take her criminal scheme into the Oval Office."[16] Clinton campaign chairman John Podesta harshly criticized Comey's letter:

> It is extraordinary that we would see something like this just 11 days out from a presidential election. The Director owes it to the American people to immediately provide the full details of what he is now examining. We are confident this will not produce any conclusions different from the one the FBI reached in July.[17]

The gap in the polls began to narrow.

CHAPTER EIGHT

A NOVEMBER
SURPRISE

Just two days before the election, FBI director Comey had another announcement to make. The FBI had completed its search of the new e-mails. Comey said, "Based on our review, we have not changed our conclusions that we expressed in July with respect to Secretary Clinton."[1]

The Clinton and Trump campaigns reacted very differently to the news. "We were always confident nothing would cause the July decision to be revisited," said Clinton's press secretary, Brian Fallon. "Now, Director Comey has confirmed it."[2]

Trump reacted angrily, insisting that the FBI was protecting Clinton and hiding evidence against her. In fact, Trump announced, the entire election was

Clinton, *left*, and an aide arrive at an airport in Cleveland on November 6, 2016, following the release of Comey's letter.

MORE TO THE
STORY

CARDING THE VOTERS

After the 2012 election, many Republicans brought up the issue of voter fraud. They claimed ineligible voters were going to the polls and casting illegal ballots. They said some voters were showing up more than once to vote. If no identification was required, they said, such fraud was easy to accomplish. In his campaign speeches, Trump announced that voter fraud was a common problem that might cheat him out of victory. There is no evidence that significant voter fraud has occurred in recent US presidential elections.

The proposed stricter voting requirements met opposition among those who saw it as an underhanded way to make it harder for people to vote, particularly for groups who tend to support Democrats, including the poor and racial minorities. Many states passed stricter laws anyway. In order to vote, citizens would now have to show some form of government-issued photo ID: a driver's license, for example, or a passport. In addition, the name and address on the ID must match that given on a voter registration form.

If a hopeful voter did not have proper ID, some states allowed him or her to sign an affidavit then vote as usual. This affidavit is a promise that the voter is not lying about his identity. Other states only allowed a provisional ballot, not to be counted unless the voter followed up with proof of identity. States that required a provisional ballot in 2016 included Georgia, Indiana, Kansas, Mississippi, Tennessee, Virginia, and Wisconsin.

rigged against him. The nationwide polls—which showed him down by a significant margin—were showing false results, he said. He claimed that on November 8 fraudulent voting would skew the vote tallies against him. He did not provide any evidence pointing to the possibility of widespread fraud.

RIGGED ELECTIONS?

Trump had already brought up the topic of a rigged election. He claimed the government and media were conspiring to cheat him of victory. "The election is absolutely being rigged by the dishonest and distorted media pushing Crooked Hillary—but also at many polling places. SAD," he tweeted out in the middle of October.[3] Trump also implied in speeches and interviews that he may not accept the results of the election if he lost. He would contest the results by demanding recounts and filing lawsuits.

The country had already gone through a close election that was finally decided in the courts. It happened in 2000, when Democratic candidate Al Gore faced Republican nominee George W. Bush. A close vote in the swing state

Worries about a contested election evoked memories of the 2000 election between George W. Bush, *left*, and Al Gore, *right*.

of Florida led to a recount of votes, which dragged on for several weeks while the nation waited. Finally, lawyers working for the Republican campaign filed a lawsuit to stop the recount. The decision in the case was appealed to the Supreme Court, which finally stopped the recount and awarded the election to Bush—despite the fact that Gore had won the final popular vote tally.

Politicians on both sides were not eager to repeat the experience of 2000 and the Florida recount. Trump's running mate, Pence, tried to calm the fears in an interview, saying, "We will absolutely accept the result of the election. Look, the American people will speak in an election that will culminate on November the 8th. But the American people are tired of the obvious bias in the national media. That's where the sense of a rigged election goes here."[4]

THE BIG NIGHT

More than 40 million Americans voted early, either through the mail or in person. On Tuesday, November 8, all polling places opened across the country. Election coverage began early in the evening. Using the early results, the networks began making projections of the winner. At approximately 7:00 p.m. eastern time, the AP officially made its first projections—Trump would win Indiana and Kentucky, as expected. Clinton would win the reliably Democratic state of Vermont.

Polls closed later in the Midwest and western United States. By 10:30, Trump had

THE LEGEND OF DIXVILLE NOTCH

There isn't much in the news about Dixville Notch, New Hampshire. It's a small town with a population of 20 or so near the Canadian border. But every four years, right around Election Day, this quiet city reappears in the headlines. It's the first town in the country to vote, just after midnight on the day of the election. It's also the first voting precinct to report results.

The results don't always predict the election. In 2000, 2004, and 2008, Dixville Notchers went for the winner, but in 2012 they split 5-5 for Barack Obama and Mitt Romney. In 2016, Hillary Clinton won the Dixville Notch vote by a landslide: four votes to two. Gary Johnson of the Libertarian Party took one additional vote, and another voter submitted Mitt Romney as a write-in choice.[5]

been declared the winner of Ohio. After the Ohio result, the swing states started to fall for Trump, with Florida and North Carolina going Republican. The path to 270 votes became easier for Trump. Clinton's hopes hung on the states of Wisconsin, Michigan, and Pennsylvania.

The night before the election, Clinton had made her final appearance in Philadelphia, Pennsylvania's largest city. Her campaign saw the state as a crucial part of the Democratic firewall—the collection of solidly Democratic states—that would bring her to the White House. But a victory in Pennsylvania gave Trump 264 electoral votes, just six short of the total he needed.

WATCHING OHIO

Presidential campaigns always pay close attention to Ohio. This crucial swing state has voted for the eventual winner in every presidential election since 1964. Ohio has also sent a large number of its politicians to the White House. Ulysses S. Grant, Rutherford B. Hayes, James A. Garfield, Benjamin Harrison, William McKinley, William Howard Taft, and Warren G. Harding all hailed from Ohio.

As each voting precinct and county declared its winner, the video maps on broadcast and cable news lit up red (Republican) or blue (Democratic). The tallies around 2:00 a.m. were still close in Wisconsin, Michigan, and

Arizona. Trump needed only one of these states to win the election.

The vote-counting dragged into the early morning hours. At 2:30 a.m., the media finally declared Wisconsin a win for Trump. This put him over the 270-vote threshold needed for victory.

Soon afterward, Clinton called Trump to concede defeat and congratulate him. Trump then appeared before a crowd of happy supporters to announce the results. He praised Clinton for her service to the country and promised a successful presidency:

> Every single American will have the opportunity to realize his or her fullest potential. The forgotten men and women of our country will be forgotten no longer. We are going to fix our inner cities and rebuild our highways, bridges, tunnels, airports, schools, hospitals. We're going to rebuild our infrastructure, which will become, by the way, second to none. And we will put millions of our people to work as we rebuild it.[6]

Trump delivered his victory speech onstage in New York City alongside his family members.

On the morning of Wednesday, November 9, those who went to bed before the result woke up to unexpected news. Trump, who was trailing Clinton by several percentage points in the final opinion polls, had won the presidency with a margin of approximately 80 electoral votes. But the popular vote tally told a different story. Clinton had defeated Trump by approximately 2.8 million votes.[7] In the simultaneous Congressional elections, both the Senate and the House of Representatives ended up with Republican majorities.

HOW IT HAPPENED

As they sorted through the results, media commentators came up with several theories as to how Trump pulled off the win. Certainly the swing state

THIRD-PARTY TALLIES

Although more than two candidates appeared on the presidential ballot in 2016, only Clinton and Trump had a serious chance to win. That didn't stop Gary Johnson of the Libertarian Party or Jill Stein of the Green Party from staging national campaigns. These candidates held themselves out to voters as true alternatives to big-party politics. Although they weren't allowed to take part in the debates, they still made headlines and attracted voters.

The final tally on November 8 was 4,489,233 votes for Johnson, or 3.27 percent of the total votes cast, and 1,457,222 for Stein, or 1.06 percent of the total.[8] In several states, these third-party candidates may have changed the outcome. In Michigan, Wisconsin, and Pennsylvania, for example, Stein won more votes than the final difference between Trump and Clinton. Election experts believe this may have cost Clinton those states' electoral votes and thus the victory.

victories were essential, as much of the Democratic firewall for Clinton held in place. New York, Illinois, California, and Minnesota all went for Clinton, as did the entire New England region, Virginia, Colorado, and Nevada. But Trump pulled out victories in Michigan (by 0.3 percent), Florida (by 1.4 percent), Wisconsin (by 0.6 percent), Ohio (by 8.6 percent), and Pennsylvania (by 1.3 percent).[9] The Republican needed most of these swing states for a win. If approximately 100,000 votes in Michigan, Wisconsin, and Florida had gone the other way, Clinton would have won the electoral college.[10]

Another viewpoint held that the voters were truly angry with the status quo in Washington. They weren't very enthusiastic about returning Clinton to the White House. According to this view, an outsider would be just the medicine needed to cure Washington's perceived ills.

"IT'S CLEAR THAT LARGE NUMBERS OF WHITE, WORKING-CLASS VOTERS SHIFTED FROM THE DEMOCRATS TO MR. TRUMP. OVERALL, ALMOST ONE IN FOUR OF PRESIDENT OBAMA'S 2012 WHITE WORKING-CLASS SUPPORTERS DEFECTED FROM THE DEMOCRATS IN 2016."[11]

—NATE COHN IN THE *NEW YORK TIMES*

FROM THE
HEADLINES

THE 2016 ELECTORAL MAP

The standard electoral map of 2016 shows Trump winning in Republican strongholds through the South, the Great Plains, and the Mountain states (except for Colorado and New Mexico). Hillary took the reliably Democratic New England, the mid-Atlantic region, the Pacific coast states, and the Midwestern states of Illinois and Minnesota. The main difference from the elections of 2008 and 2012 were swing states that went Republican in 2016, including Michigan, Wisconsin, Pennsylvania, and Ohio.

The map shows red (Republican-voting) states

WA 12
MT 3
OR 7
ID 4
WY 3
NV 6
UT 6
CO 9
CA 55
AZ 11
NM 5
AK 3

dominating through the middle of the country and the South. Blue (Democratic-voting) states line the coasts. In general, Trump won where there were fewer people—the rural states—while Clinton took the cities. This has been a trend between Democratic and Republican candidates in elections for several decades.

MAINE'S 2ND CONGRESSIONAL DISTRICT 1

ND 3
MN 10
SD 3
WI 10
MI 16
VT 3
ME 3
NH 4
NY 29
MA 11
RI 4
NE 5
IA 6
IL 20
IN 11
OH 18
PA 20
NJ 14
CT 7
KS 6
MO 10
KY 8
WV 5
VA 13
DE 3
MD 10
WASHINGTON, DC 3
OK 7
AR 6
TN 11
NC 15
SC 9
MS 6
AL 9
GA 16
TX 38
LA 8
FL 29
HI 4

■ STATES CLINTON WON

■ STATES TRUMP WON

91

CHAPTER NINE

THE
DAY AFTER

O n the morning of November 9, Clinton appeared at the gathering of her supporters at the Javits Center in New York. It had been a long night for everyone involved, but she had found the energy for a final campaign speech—to concede defeat. She spoke to the people who had passionately supported her historic campaign and who might have seen her as a role model: "To all the little girls who are watching this, never doubt that you are valuable and powerful and deserving of every chance and opportunity in the world to pursue and achieve your own dreams."[1]

As presidential candidates losing elections usually do, she praised the American tradition of peacefully transferring power to the winner. She urged her voters

Clinton was flanked at her concession speech by her husband, Bill, *left*, and her running mate, Tim Kaine, *right*.

to respect the democratic process and give Trump a chance. "Donald Trump is going to be our president," she declared. "I hope that he will be a successful president for all Americans. . . . We owe him an open mind and a chance to lead."[2]

The Trump team prepared for the long transition. The inauguration of a new president takes place on January 20 of the year following an election. That gives the president-elect two-and-a-half months to appoint the people who will staff the White House and serve as his advisers. Approximately 4,000 jobs in the federal government are appointed by the president.[3]

The election itself has one more event to make it official. On December 19, electors met in each state capital to cast their ballots. Each is bound to vote for the candidate he or she is pledged to, whether it's Trump or Clinton. The popular vote winner in the state determines which electors may cast their ballots. But the result is known, and the vote is a legal formality.

Trump's election was a surprise to leaders around the world. Following the polls, they were confident that Clinton would be the next American president. Although these polls had given Clinton a slim lead of three or four points, many were wrong in the crucial swing states. The RealClearPolitics website, which shows the results of all state and national polls, averaged six separate polls in the days just before the election. This showed Clinton winning by 46.8 to 43.6 percent—a spread quite close to the actual popular vote margin (Clinton 48.2 to Trump 46.1).[5]

QUESTIONING THE POLLS

Several polls were way off base, however. Several theories to explain this were put forth. Some believed that Trump voters were reluctant to admit their support to strangers over the phone. The British politician

FAITHLESS ELECTORS

The final voting for the 2016 election took place on December 19. In most states, the law requires electors to vote for their pledged candidate. But electors don't always follow the rules. These people, known as faithless electors, change their votes. This is usually rare, and it has never changed the outcome of an election.

The election of 2016 had multiple unfaithful electors. In Texas, Trump lost one elector to John Kasich, and another to Ron Paul. One Hawaiian elector voted for Bernie Sanders. In Washington, where Clinton took the popular vote, three of her electors wrote in the name of former US Army general and secretary of state Colin Powell. Another voted for activist Faith Spotted Eagle, who became the first Native American in history to earn an electoral vote for president. In Minnesota, where the law requires electors to vote according to their pledge, a faithless elector was dismissed and replaced. As a result, in 2016 seven electoral votes went where they weren't supposed to go—an all-time record number of faithless electors.[4]

Nigel Farage, an ally of Trump, claimed that polls were not surveying people who had not voted in recent elections. If a candidate can turn out new voters, or those discouraged by elections in the past, then he or she can achieve an unexpected victory.

Trump himself had a theory: the polls were rigged by Hillary supporters. Those who managed the polling supported his opponent, and they were fudging the results to show him behind Clinton. Trump held to this theory even as he was preparing for the inauguration in January 2017. In a tweet sent out on January 17, he claimed, "The same people who did the phony election polls, and were so wrong, are now doing approval rating polls. They are rigged just like before."[6]

Trump presented no evidence for this assertion. He was responding to polls showing him with the lowest approval rating of any new president at the time of the inauguration. The polling group CNN/ORC, for example,

"I'M TOLD THAT NEW REGISTRATION OF VOTERS IS QUITE HIGH. IT COULD BE THAT HILLARY'S AHEAD, BUT MAYBE BY NOT SO MUCH."[8]

—NIGEL FARAGE, DAYS BEFORE THE ELECTION

showed the president-elect with a 40 percent approval rating, down six points from the day of the election.[7]

Trump had indeed overcome a widespread expectation that Clinton would easily win. Media critics pointed out that the focus on scandal and personal attacks showed Trump constantly under fire for one misstep or another. This may have created an impression that Trump had little chance in the general election. Trump supporters, however, weren't deterred by Trump's character. They saw the media as biased against him, and they wanted a different kind of president anyway. Many Republicans may have simply voted for their party rather than supporting the specific candidate.

A DIFFERENT ELECTION

The election of 2016 had been long and surprising. From the time of his first announcement, Trump had defied the general opinion: as a political novice, he was seen as having no chance to win. At first, more experienced candidates in the Republican Party had not taken his campaign very seriously. They couldn't quite envision a newcomer winning the first campaign he had ever

run—a campaign for the highest office in the nation. On the Democratic side, Clinton had made history as the first woman to be selected as the nominee from a major party. Her message resonated with voters who wanted social and economic fairness, environmental protection, and the experience of someone with a long political history.

By running against the establishment in Washington, however, Trump mined a rich vein of discontent with the political system. While enjoying powerful and well paid positions in the capital, Republicans and Democrats were perceived as having lost touch with the needs of the voters. In the Midwestern swing states that delivered the win to Trump, the loss of jobs and stagnant economic conditions prompted voters to take a chance on someone completely different.

Anti-Trump protests sprung up around the country between the election and the inauguration.

ESSENTIAL
FACTS

MAJOR EVENTS

- The 2016 presidential campaign kicks off with the Iowa caucuses on February 1. Caucuses as well as primary votes open to the general public continue through early June.

- In July 2016, the two major parties convene their presidential nominating conventions. The Republican Party, meeting in Cleveland, nominates Donald Trump. The Democrats hold their convention the following week in Philadelphia and nominate Hillary Clinton.

- The presidential election on Tuesday, November 8, results in Trump winning important swing states, including Pennsylvania, Florida, Ohio, Wisconsin, and Michigan, as well as a majority of electoral votes. Although she has won a majority of the popular vote, Clinton concedes defeat in a 2:30 a.m. phone call to Trump.

KEY PLAYERS

- Hillary Clinton was the Democratic nominee for president.

- Donald Trump was the Republican nominee for president and won the election.

- Mike Pence was the Republican vice presidential candidate.

- Tim Kaine was the Democratic vice presidential candidate.

IMPACT ON SOCIETY

The 2016 presidential election delivered the presidency as well as majorities in the House of Representatives and the Senate to the Republican Party. The election was closely contested, with controversies over the use of a private e-mail server by Hillary Clinton, assistance to the Trump campaign from Russian hackers, Trump's remarks about women and minorities, and the role of the FBI in swaying public opinion. The electoral college also came into the spotlight with the ultimate winner of the electoral vote failing to win a majority of votes among the public.

QUOTES

"It's outrageous that multi-millionaires and billionaires are allowed to play by a different set of rules than hardworking families, especially when it comes to paying their fair share of taxes."

—Hillary Clinton, January 11, 2016

"Nobody knows the system better than me, which is why I alone can fix it."

—Donald Trump, July 21, 2016

GLOSSARY

AMENDMENT

A formal addition or change to a document.

BROKERED CONVENTION

A nominating convention in which no candidate reaches a majority on the first ballot, thus forcing further ballots until the party finally elects its nominee.

CAUCUS

A meeting of party members, who discuss the candidates, listen to speeches, and cast ballots for their favorites.

DELEGATE

A person sent to a convention to represent a group or a state.

ENDORSEMENT

An announcement of support of a candidate by another politician or by a media outlet such as a newspaper.

INDEPENDENT

A candidate not affiliated with a political party.

PLATFORM

The policies of a political party.

PRECINCT

A voting district of a city or town.

PRIMARY

A contest political parties hold to determine their presidential nominees.

TRANSITION

The period between the election and the inauguration of the new president on January 20 of the following year.

ADDITIONAL
RESOURCES

SELECTED BIBLIOGRAPHY

Bordo, Susan. *The Destruction of Hillary Clinton.* Brooklyn, NY: Melville, 2017. Print.

Lake, Thomas. *Unprecedented: The Election That Changed Everything.* New York: Melcher, 2017. Print.

FURTHER READINGS

Carser, A. R. *Donald Trump: 45th US President.* Minneapolis, MN: Abdo, 2017. Print.

Cummings, Judy Dodge. *Hillary Clinton: Groundbreaking Politician.* Minneapolis, MN: Abdo, 2017. Print.

ONLINE RESOURCES

To learn more about the 2016 presidential election, visit **abdobooklinks.com**. These links are routinely monitored and updated to provide the most current information available.

MORE INFORMATION

For more information on this subject, contact or visit the following organizations:

US Capitol Visitor Center
United States Capitol
Washington, DC 20510
202-226-8000
visitthecapitol.gov
This office assists individuals and groups in touring the Capitol building in Washington, DC.

The White House
1600 Pennsylvania Avenue
Washington, DC 20500
whitehouse.gov
The official residence of the president is open for self-guided tours by submitting a request through a congressional representative.

SOURCE
NOTES

CHAPTER 1. TWO PARTIES IN NEW YORK

1. Jamie Turner. "Election Night 2016: Donald Trump Becomes President Elect." *Cleveland.com*. Cleveland.com, 9 Nov. 2016. Web. 14 Aug. 2017.

2. Ari Berman. "There Are 868 Fewer Places to Vote in 2016 Because the Supreme Court Gutted the Voting Rights Act." *Nation*. Nation, 4 Nov. 2016. Web. 14 Aug. 2017.

3. Brian Stelter. "In Their Own Words: The Story of Covering Election Night 2016." *CNN*. CNN, 5 Jan. 2017. Web. 14 Aug. 2017.

CHAPTER 2. RIDING THE GOLDEN ESCALATOR

1. "Here's Donald Trump's Presidential Announcement Speech." *Time*. Time, 16 June 2015. Web. 14 Aug. 2017.

2. Ibid.

3. "Full Text: Donald Trump Announces a Presidential Bid." *Washington Post*. Washington Post, 16 June 2015. Web. 14 Aug. 2017.

4. Patrick Reis. "16 Falsehoods Spewed by Trump and Clinton." *Politico*. Politico, 6 Nov. 2016. Web. 14 Aug. 2017.

5. Ewen MacAskill. "Donald Trump Bows out of 2012 US Presidential Election Race." *Guardian*. Guardian, 16 May 2011. Web. 14 Aug. 2017.

6. Pamela Engel. "How Trump Came Up with His Slogan 'Make America Great Again.'" *Business Insider*. Business Insider, 18 Jan. 2017. Web. 14 Aug. 2017.

7. "Make America Great Again – Trademark Details." *Justia Trademarks*. Justia, 14 July 2015. Web. 14 Aug. 2017.

CHAPTER 3. THE FRONT-RUNNER

1. "Hillary Clinton Uses YouTube Video to Announce She Is Running for President." *Telegraph*. Telegraph, 12 Apr. 2015. Web. 14 Aug. 2017.

2. "A Fair Tax System." *HillaryClinton.com*. HillaryClinton.com, n.d. Web. 14 Aug. 2017.

3. "The 6 Questions Hillary Clinton Answered in Iowa." *Des Moines Register*. Des Moines Register, 20 May 2015. Web. 14 Aug. 2017.

4. "Super PACs." *Open Secrets*. Center for Responsive Politics, n.d. Web. 14 Aug. 2017.

CHAPTER 4. THE PRIMARY SEASON

1. David Weigel. "Iowa Caucuses: Here's How the Voting Works." *Washington Post*. Washington Post, 1 Feb. 2016. Web. 14 Aug. 2017.

2. Stephen Collinson. "The Iowa Caucuses, Explained." *CNN*. CNN, 2 Feb. 2016. Web. 14 Aug. 2017.

3. "Results from the 2016 Iowa Caucus." *Wall Street Journal*. Wall Street Journal, 1 Feb. 2016. Web. 14 Aug. 2017.

4. Robert Yoon. "$153 Million in Bill and Hillary Clinton Speaking Fees, Documented." *CNN*. CNN, 6 Feb. 2016. Web. 14 Aug. 2017.

5. Ben Geier. "Speech Inflation: Why Bill Clinton, George W. Bush, and Others Get Massive Speaking Fees." *Fortune*. Fortune, 11 June 2015. Web. 14 Aug. 2017.

6. Daniel Gross. "Stop Freaking Out Over Obama's $400,000 Speaking Fee." *Slate*. Slate, 26 Apr. 2017. Web. 14 Aug. 2017.

7. Tim Devaney. "Rubio: 'Gang of 8' Immigration Bill Never Meant to Pass." *Hill*. Hill, 15 Feb. 2016. Web. 14 Aug. 2017.

8. Arnie Seipel. "With Primary Season in Final Stretch, Sanders Reports Slowed Fundraising." *NPR*. NPR, 1 May 2016. Web. 14 Aug. 2017.

9. Drew DeSilver. "Who Are the Democratic Superdelegates?" *Factank*. Pew Research Center, 5 May 2016. Web. 14 Aug. 2017.

10. Jessica Taylor. "As Cruz Exits Race, Trump Cements His Spot as Likely GOP Nominee." *NPR*. NPR, 3 May 2016. Web. 14 Aug. 2017.

11. Deirdre Walsh and Manu Raju. "Paul Ryan Rips Donald Trump Remarks as 'Textbook Definition of a Racist Comment.'" *CNN*. CNN, 7 June 2016. Web. 14 Aug. 2017.

12. Kristina Davis. "Trump University Litigation Gears Up for Final Showdown Thursday." *San Diego Union-Tribune*. San Diego Union-Tribune, 30 Mar. 2017. Web. 14 Aug. 2017.

13. Jessica Taylor. "As Cruz Exits Race, Trump Cements His Spot as Likely GOP Nominee." *NPR*. NPR, 3 May 2016. Web. 14 Aug. 2017.

CHAPTER 5. THE CONVENTIONS

1. David Frum. "GOP's Worst Nightmare—A Contested Convention." *CNN*. CNN, 20 Feb. 2012. Web. 14 Aug. 2017.

2. Ben Schreckinger. "Trump Attacks McCain: 'I Like People Who Weren't Captured.'" *Politico*. Politico, 18 July 2015. Web. 14 Aug. 2017.

3. Bill Rehkopf. "Full Speech: Ted Cruz Addresses Republican Convention Delegates." *Hill*. Hill, 20 July 2016. Web. 14 Aug. 2017.

4. "Full Text: Donald Trump 2016 RNC Draft Speech Transcript." *Politico*. Politico, 21 July 2016. Web. 14 Aug. 2017.

5. "Full Text: Khizr Khan's Speech to the 2016 Democratic National Convention." *ABC News*. ABC News, 1 Aug. 2016. Web. 14 Aug. 2017.

6. "Remarks at the Democratic National Convention." *HillaryClinton.com*. HillaryClinton.com, 29 July 2016. Web. 14 Aug. 2017.

7. "Fact Check: Hillary Clinton's Speech to the Democratic Convention, Annotated." *NPR*. NPR, 28 July 2016. Web. 14 Aug. 2017.

8. Aaron Blake. "Here Are the Latest, Most Damaging Things in the DNC's Leaked Emails." *Washington Post*. Washington Post, 25 July 2016. Web. 14 Aug. 2017.

SOURCE NOTES
CONTINUED

CHAPTER 6. THE GENERAL CAMPAIGN

1. "Donald Trump Speech, Debates and Campaign Quotes." *Newsday*. Newsday, 9 Nov. 2016. Web. 14 Aug. 2017.

2. Tim Mak. "Donald Trump Bungles Hillary Clinton's Tax Returns Attack." *Daily Beast*. Daily Beast, 26 Sept. 2016. Web. 14 Aug. 2017.

3. Amy Chozick and Steve Eder. "Foundation Ties Bedevil Hillary Clinton's Presidential Campaign." *New York Times*. New York Times, 20 Aug. 2016. Web. 14 Aug. 2017.

CHAPTER 7. STATUS QUO VERSUS UPSTART

1. Katie Zezima and Matthew Callahan. "Donald Trump vs. Hillary Clinton on the Issues." *Washington Post*. Washington Post, 23 Sept. 2016. Web. 14 Aug. 2017.

2. "Presidential Debates (2015–2016)." *Ballotpedia*. Ballotpedia, 20 Oct. 2016. Web. 14 Aug. 2017.

3. Aaron Blake. "The First Trump-Clinton Presidential Debate Transcript, Annotated." *Washington Post*. Washington Post, 26 Sept. 2016. Web. 14 Aug. 2017.

4. "Full Transcript: First 2016 Presidential Debate." *Politico*. Politico, 27 Sept. 2016. Web. 14 Aug. 2017.

5. Ibid.

6. Aaron Blake. "Everything That Was Said at the Second Donald Trump vs. Hillary Clinton Debate, Highlighted." *Washington Post*. Washington Post, 9 Oct. 2016. Web. 14 Aug. 2017.

7. Eric Bradner. "Melania Trump: Donald Trump Was 'Egged On' into 'Boy Talk.'" *CNN*. CNN, 18 Oct. 2016. Web. 14 Aug. 2017.

8. "Transcript of the Second Debate." *New York Times*. New York Times, 10 Oct. 2016. Web. 14 Aug. 2017.

9. Ibid.

10. Aaron Blake. "The Final Trump-Clinton Debate Transcript, Annotated." *Washington Post*. Washington Post, 19 Oct. 2016. Web. 14 Aug. 2017.

11. "Full Transcript: Third 2016 Presidential Debate." *Politico*. Politico, 20 Oct. 2016. Web. 14 Aug. 2017.

12. Donovan Slack and Eliza Collins. "How We Got Here: A Timeline of the Clinton Email Scandal." *USA Today*. USA Today, 6 Nov. 2016. Web. 14 Aug. 2017.

13. "Statement by FBI Director James B. Comey." *FBI*. FBI, 5 July 2016. Web. 14 Aug. 2017.

14. Michael Crowley and Tyler Pager. "Trump Urges Russia to Hack Clinton's Email." *Politico*. Politico, 27 July 2016. Web. 14 Aug. 2017.

15. Abigail Tracy. "FBI Renews Clinton Investigation." *Vanity Fair*. Vanity Fair, 28 Oct. 2016. Web. 14 Aug. 2017.

16. Cooper Allen and Kevin Johnson. "New Emails under Review in Clinton Case Emerged from Weiner Probe." *USA Today*. USA Today, 29 Oct. 2016. Web. 14 Aug. 2017.

17. "Statement from John Podesta in Response to FBI Letter to Congressional Chairmen." *HillaryClinton.com*. HillaryClinton.com, 28 Oct. 2016. Web. 14 Aug. 2017.

CHAPTER 8. A NOVEMBER SURPRISE

1. David Lauter. "FBI Has Reviewed New Emails, 'Not Changed Our Conclusion' on Clinton, Comey Says." *L. A. Times*. L. A. Times, 6 Nov. 2016. Web. 14 Aug. 2017.

2. Ibid.

3. Jeremy Diamond and Eugene Scott. "Trump Ratchets Up 'Rigged Election' Claims, Which Pence Downplays." *CNN*. CNN, 17 Oct. 2016. Web. 14 Aug. 2017.

4. Ibid.

5. Gregory Krieg and Sonia Moghe. "Hillary Clinton Wins Dixville Notch Midnight Vote." *CNN*. CNN, 8 Nov. 2016. Web. 14 Aug. 2017.

6. "Transcript: Donald Trump's Victory Speech." *New York Times*. New York Times, 9 Nov. 2016. Web. 14 Aug. 2017.

7. "2016 Popular Vote Tracker." *Cook Political Report*. Cook Political Report, 3 Jan. 2017. Web. 14 Aug. 2017.

8. "Official 2016 Presidential General Election Results." *FEC*. FEC, 30 Jan. 2017. Web. 14 Aug. 2017.

9. Nicholas Loffredo. "State-by-State Presidential Election Results." *Newsweek*. Newsweek, 8 Nov. 2016. Web. 14 Aug. 2017.

10. Tim Meko, Denise Lu, and Lazaro Gamio. "How Trump Won the Presidency with Razor-Thin Margins in Swing States." *Washington Post*. Washington Post, 11 Nov. 2016. Web. 14 Aug. 2017.

11. Nate Cohn. "A 2016 Review: Turnout Wasn't the Driver of Clinton's Defeat." *Upshot*. New York Times, 28 Mar. 2017. Web. 14 Aug. 2017.

CHAPTER 9. THE DAY AFTER

1. Katie Reilly. "Read Hillary Clinton's Concession Speech for the 2016 Presidential Election." *Time*. Time, 9 Nov. 2016. Web. 14 Aug. 2017.

2. Ibid.

3. Zach Piaker. "Help Wanted: 4,000 Presidential Appointees." *Center for Presidential Transition*. Center for Presidential Transition, 16 Mar. 2016. Web. 14 Aug. 2017.

4. Kiersten Schmidt and Wilson Andrews. "A Historic Number of Electors Defected, and Most Were Supposed to Vote for Clinton." *New York Times*. New York Times, 19 Dec. 2016.

5. "Pennsylvania: Trump vs. Clinton." *RealClearPolitics*. RealClearPolitics, n.d. Web. 14 Aug. 2017.

6. "Donald J. Trump." *Twitter*. Twitter, 17 Jan. 2017. Web. 14 Aug. 2017.

7. Elliot Smilowitz. "Trump: Approval Polls Are Rigged against Me." *Hill*. Hill, 17 Jan. 2017. Web. 14 Aug. 2017.

8. Richard Allen Greene. "Trump vs. Clinton: Could the Polls Be Wrong?" *CNN*. CNN, 8 Nov. 2016. Web. 14 Aug. 2017.

INDEX

ABOUT THE
AUTHOR

Tom Streissguth is the author of more than 100 books for young readers on history, current affairs, science, and geography. He is also the founder of The Archive, a publisher of historic journalism by major American authors including Mark Twain, Jack London, and Ernest Hemingway. He has worked as a teacher, book editor, and journalist, and has traveled widely in Europe, the Middle East, and Southeast Asia. He currently lives in Woodbury, Minnesota.